Life and Leadership
Pure and Simple!

Life and Leadership Pure and Simple!

A Common Sense Approach

Steven C. Duncan

Copyright © 2017 Steven C. Duncan
All rights reserved.

ISBN: 1541233379
ISBN 13: 9781541233379
Library of Congress Control Number: 2016921351
CreateSpace Independent Publishing Platform
North Charleston, South Carolina

Introduction

"Common sense" is a phrase used quite often by many and a trait shared by nearly every individual to some degree. However, good commonsense practices are often overlooked in favor of obtained knowledge or learned behaviors. We acquire some of these behaviors at an early age, and they stay with us our entire lives. We get trapped by our own thought process when we look at those things that appear to be obvious, and we will readily accept the prescription. I'm sure that you've heard the phrase "It is what it is"; however, I say, "Not so fast!"

The intent of this book is to provide a straightforward assessment of common sense and explore the dimensions of good commonsense practices, the use of guiding principles, and the practical application surrounding this subject both personally and professionally.

The goal is to move the needle beyond the obvious in the thought process and dig deeper to gain better knowledge and understanding regarding any situation. We need to move beyond our emotional habits to an area where proactive discipline is dominant instead of reactive responses.

The aforementioned is especially true for modern leaders. Today's leaders have a unique opportunity to influence and shape the future of society and our nation. In the world of business, media, or politics, the ability to deploy a good commonsense strategy regarding true leadership is of the utmost importance if we are to remain a world leader in any of these fields of endeavor.

Moreover, it is today's leaders who are the standard bearers for the future generation of leaders who will undeniably come. This is arguably one of the most important quests of our time. In the age of the Internet and social media, information moves rapidly, so much so that the ability to comprehend more than the obvious often gets suppressed by the sheer deluge of information; thus, good common sense from a broader perspective receives little if any consideration. Ultimately, this transitions our commonsense thought process to a reactive mode rather than a proactive position with regards to the way we view the issues and challenges we face in everyday life.

Therefore, as we move through the chapters in this book, it is important to reflect on life's journey and adjust our emotional attitudes. We need to be willing to pause and think about those issues and challenges we encounter along the journey—hence, the subtitle of this book: *A Commonsense Approach*.

...Let's begin.

Contents

    Introduction ························ v

I   Common Sense: Opening Discussion, Part 1 ········ 1
II   Common Sense: Opening Discussion, Part 2 ········ 7
III The Today Principle ······················ 11
IV The Balance Principle ····················· 19
V   The Existence Principle ···················· 26
VI The Employee-Contributor Principle ··········· 33
VII The Seek-and-Find Principle ················ 36
VIII The Visionary Principle···················· 43
IX The R-E-S-P-E-C-T Principle ················ 51
X   The Positive Principle····················· 58
XI The Thread Principle ····················· 69
XII The Beginning Principle ··················· 76
XIII The Noise-Pollution Principle ··············· 85
XIV A Closing Message ······················ 91

    References························· 95
    About the Author······················ 97

I

Common Sense: Opening Discussion, Part 1

When we explore the traditional meaning of "leadership," we find many definitions ranging from interpersonal skills to political behavior. Throughout my career, I have heard many people say that there is no quick fix regarding the approach to becoming an effective leader. Perhaps this is true to some degree; however, there is one trait that connects the dots as it relates to every leadership discipline imaginable, which is appropriately known as **common sense**. As we move through this book, we will explore methods, ideas, and the conceptual applications of good commonsense attributes and practices.

Before we dive into the discussion, there is one burning question: What is common sense? Is it a learned behavior? A trait that we inherit? Is it something that we're born with? Or is it a mind-set we develop from life experiences?

Perhaps each of these questions has merit; however, one thing is clear: common sense is an attribute that requires constant nurturing and is one of the single most important attributes for leaders not only to master but also to adhere to.

This statement can be qualified on many fronts. Today, when we explore the backdrop of politics, business, and even personal endeavors, the ability to use good common sense as it relates to practical matters appears to elude most individuals. In other words, good commonsense practices and principles have ceased to exist or have a position in our daily lives.

Some may consider this a pretty bold statement, right? Absolutely! Case in point:

1. In the world of politics, many followers pledge an allegiance to a particular political party, political group, or party leader. These followers will passionately declare that they are staunch Democrats, Republicans, or Independents without giving any consideration to the agenda of the party they are so passionately loyal to or their party leader; however, the greater question is *why*. Does this loyalty stem from individual upbringing? Does it stem from something that was learned or experienced? Does it simply stem from an established position or attitude?

2. In the world of business, many business leaders, regardless of their level within the organization, have been faced with ethical behavior conducive to personal failure and/or the demise of the organization. From a personal perspective, I once worked for a firm that at one time was one of the largest same-day logistic carriers nationwide. This firm had a very strong business model from the outset, but as years passed, shady business practices and driver pay issues started the downward spiral of this organization. The firm began to suffer massive financial losses and years later went out of business.

Speaking frankly, when I was a member of management at this nameless firm, on several occasions, the facility where I was assigned faced eviction for nonpayment of rent and utility cut-off notices. Driver settlements would be short-paid nearly every week, and some drivers would go weeks without being properly compensated. From a managerial perspective, these and other developments were nothing short of frustrating.

The following statement may appear contemptuous, but I can passionately state, with no regrets, my proudest moment at the firm was the day I left.

A pretty sad indictment but, again, the greatest question still remains: *why*? How can a firm engage in such ethical misconduct? Why would leadership engage in practices that deprived drivers of receiving their hard-earned pay? Why let monthly bills go unpaid only to receive threats of eviction and utility shut-off notices?

In truth, these questions speak to the ability to use good commonsense practices on a large scale, but, conversely, the principles of good commonsense theories and applications apply to us all.

I have conducted brief interviews with many individuals regarding their personal definition of "common sense." I've found that when you ask this question, you'll receive a wide range of answers:

- Some believe that it's a trait learned during our upbringing.
- Some believe that it's a mental process.
- Some believe that you either have it or you don't.
- Some believe that it's a phenomenon of human existence.

The list could go on and on, but I find it fascinating that when you ask this question, you get different answers—very widespread and all over the map, if you will.

Considering all of the various answers received from these interviews, there is one thing that is quite clear: common sense is a subject that requires greater understanding, research, and discussion.

Therefore, I believe that common sense has academic potential, particularly as a curriculum from middle school to the undergraduate and/or graduate levels of education. This subject should not be blended with your traditional psychology or cognitive-thinking class. Common sense is an entity that has merits in and of itself. The subject of common sense unequivocally has the ability to generate much discussion and immense research. As we move through this book, my hope is that you'll find a convincing argument regarding the need to install common sense at the academic level.

II

Common Sense: Opening Discussion, Part 2

There are in fact many attributes essential to developing good leadership skills that cannot be ignored. Novice and tenured leaders alike must possess certain skill sets to maintain an effective level of leadership. To develop or enhance leadership skills, many will attend specially designed leadership-training classes and leadership seminars. Some will even attend college to enhance their leadership skills.

Unquestionably, there are many traits and attributes essential to developing good overall leadership skills. If you are reading this book and are currently in a leadership role or aspire to be a leader, you will find that the following characteristics are fundamental to your leadership skills: honesty, competence, integrity, the ability to inspire, intelligence, fair-mindedness, broad-mindedness, courage, straightforwardness, and creativity. All are essential leadership traits; however, none are more important than possessing a high level of good common sense.

The term "common sense," in its purest form, has been around for many centuries. Aristotle, born in 384 BCE in a small town called Stagira in ancient Greece, was a philosopher and scientist who left a timeless legacy for Western philosophers and civilization. Aristotle is considered to be one of the first people to discuss common sense theory and application. Aristotle's insightful assessment of common sense offers an in-depth explanation regarding the correlation between animals and humans as it relates to the five senses and how we perceive things that we considered real or meaningful in our everyday lives.

A masterful book written by Pavel Gregoric, an associate professor at the University of Zagreb in Croatia, provides an in-depth look at Aristotle's hypothesis on common sense. This book is a brilliant piece of work by Professor Gregoric and offers a convincing assessment regarding the application of Aristotle's common sense theory. The text, *Aristotle on the Common Sense,* is published by Oxford University Press and is a must-read for any individual seeking to gain further understanding of the origins of the commonsense theories and applications.

The purpose behind capturing Aristotle's common sense hypostasis is not so much to retrace history but to reflect how long the notion of common sense has been a part of human life.

In addition, it helps us understand today's definition of common sense and how it applies to everyday life. For the purpose of discussion, our primary focus will be life and leadership.

As you can see, the term "common sense" is not some new-age phenomenon; yet it is one of the most-forgotten leadership trait. Many modern leaders tend to push aside common sense in favor of learned behavior, business-school principles, and other business-school teachings. As a progressive and civilized nation, in a competitive global market, in an environment where many next-generation leaders aspire to climb the corporate ladder, it's not very hard to surmise how common sense can often times take a backseat in favor of career goals and/or aspirations.

However, any current or future leader aspiring to be *not just good, but great* must continually practice and maintain a good commonsense approach in every aspect of leadership. Regardless of levels of education, business-school teachings, or job training, without good common sense to help guide you in an organized thought process, you could hinder or possibly stunt your potential to become a great leader or a better person.

III

The Today Principle

By modern definition, "common sense" is the "basic ability to make decisions using sound judgment." This is true; however, I submit to you an associated meaning that we will refer to as a "*Commonsense Approach.*" This is an extension of the basic definition of common sense that we can describe as:

> *"The basic ability to make decisions using sound judgment by way of an active, perpetual thought process that guides an individual through the decision-making process."*

An active, perpetual thought process works counter to *reactive* decision-making and promotes a more *proactive decision-making* process, thus leading us to a more practical approach to many of life challenges.

The commonsense approach promotes reflection and causes us to dig a little deeper and interrogate our own thought process to produce more fruitful and positive results. Moreover, the commonsense approach helps us to strike a balance in the decision-making process.

As a practical matter, common sense is a trait shared by nearly all individuals (short of any neurological disorders). Because of this trait's simplicity, many take for granted the value of using common sense in everyday matters. As previously mentioned, it is a trait that's typically abandoned when other desires and aspirations are placed in the forefront. For the sake of discussion, we will consider these desires and aspirations as "driving forces." Now there are many driving forces with regard to common sense abandonment that truly require no introduction: power, greed, money, a desire to impact change, or even political aspirations have the ability to block the common sensible. We witness evidence of this nearly every day. Here are just a few examples:

1. A police officer arrested for killing an unarmed individual
2. A politician jailed for bribery or other criminal charges
3. A teacher charged with sexual harassment or inappropriate contact with a minor
4. A corporate leader relieved of their duties for unethical business practices

These and other associate characteristics speak to an individual's inability to use good commonsense practices.

Reactive decision-making can essentially cloud one's ability to make reasonable decisions, impact the basic ability of understanding, and impede the guiding principles behind a good commonsense approach that are critical to those issues that we confront or that challenge us in our daily lives.

From a leadership perspective, when we employ good commonsense strategies, we are not guided by reactive measures or any aspiration that can prove detrimental to our career. Good commonsense leaders will typically align their decision-making process with the all-important "doing-what's-right" leadership principle. For any individual who is currently in or aspiring to a leadership role, doing what's right is undoubtedly the single most important characteristic of all leadership traits.

The doing-what's-right principle is typically a common thread found among great leaders. This attribute serves as a rudder that has the ability to guide one's conscience and heightening an awareness of the proactive decision-making process. This is particularly true in the absence of any policy and procedures or where a process has not been identified. In addition, this attribute helps to define real purpose and to avoid the pitfalls of self-serving entities and/or narcissistic behaviors.

Conversely, it's important to understand that doing what's right may not always be popular when you're in a leadership role, particularly when you consider that *what appears to be right to you may not be right in the eyes of others*. Therefore, doing what's right regarding the decision-making process requires an approach that moves beyond the obvious. To examine this statement, let's take a look at the following scenario.

Let's say that you are a manager in an organization with one hundred employees and several managers under your direct command. Over the last year, your department has been clicking on all cylinders; production has been high, and errors have been few. Your boss is very happy with your performance and your team's overall results for the year.

One day, your superiors elect to express their sincere gratitude for a job well done and present you with an award for your outstanding leadership. You are ecstatic and are very proud of the recognition.

The next day, you decide to conduct a work-group meeting with your team to share the good news and thank them for an outstanding year. You decide on an open format meeting so that your team can provide candid feedback and build on the current organizational success.

Within a week, the meeting takes place. The conference room is set with pizza and soda. After a little indulging and conversation with the team members, you get right into the meeting. You've created a PowerPoint presentation highlighting the past year's accomplishments and have developed a game plan to raise the level of performance for the upcoming fiscal year.

After your presentation, you open the floor for discussion, and to your amazement, you discover that everything is not what it had appeared to be and that all is truly not well. As your team begins to speak candidly, you start to hear unsettling and unnerving comments:

"This company doesn't care about my opinion."
"All this company cares about is the bottom line."
"I just work here to support my family."
"There is no growth and opportunity at this company."
"It's just a job; there is no real future here."

As you begin to absorb the comments by some of your team members, your once high-flying mood has been deflated like a hot-air balloon that came crashing to the ground.

After the meeting, you make your way to the nearest restroom to wash your hands, you start to rinse your eyes with a little cold water, and, as you look in the mirror at your reflection, you wonder, "What just happened?"

If you have been a leader in an organization for any length of time, perhaps you may have experienced this or a similar scenario. Undoubtedly, this situation speaks to a bigger problem within an organization; there are invisible forces at work, lying deep beneath the surface, hidden from plain view from what appears to be obvious. I can certainly attest to the aforementioned scenario, because I have personally experienced similar situations during my twenty-eight years in a leadership role.

When I was a novice manager in training, during one of the leadership-training modules, one topic that was most memorable and generated in-depth discussion was the Pareto Principle (80/20 Rule). The Pareto Principle has been widely used in business but applies to other areas such as relationships, marriage, finance, and wealth distribution.

In 1937, engineer and management consultant Joseph M. Juran adopted the Pareto Principle that was named after Italian economist Vilfredo Pareto, who surmised that 80 percent of the property in Italy was owned by 20 percent of the population in 1906.

The Pareto Principle is commonly used in business as a statistical tool to help identify problems or issues, increase production, and improve profitability. In our award-winning manager scenario, conceptually, we could adequately apply the Pareto Principle to those invisible forces that will typically fly under the radar if you are not paying attention.

Now the greater question is, "As a leader, will I be able to, or am I equipped to, satisfy my team one hundred percent of the time?" In earnest, it's highly unlikely simply because one size never fits all, and you are managing people who can be fastidious at times; however, you can satisfy the masses by deploying a good commonsense strategy in your leadership approach.

Understanding those issues that are important to people, listening to their concerns, acting upon the smallest issue, and helping others to see what's really important all play a unique role in the commonsense approach process. By doing so, you will essentially deploy the heavy equipment necessary to dig a little deeper into the problems and issues your team may not voice in a normal business setting. "No issue is too big and no problem too small" must be the impetus for today's leaders should you desire to achieve a greater measure of success.

Lastly, doing what's right is a very powerful trait that requires you to move beyond the inertia of traditional leadership principles; in other words, take nothing for granted and dig a little deeper. Moreover, doing what's right has the ability to transition you personally as well and is an important aspect regarding a sound commonsense approach to both life and leadership.

IV

The Balance Principle

In today's business world, many in leadership roles err by making corporate goals their career goals, thus neglecting the human capital necessary to run the business in the first place. Focusing solely on production quotas, managing by the numbers, or managing the bottom line will only hinder the top-level performance of any leader. The key element to achieving a superior level of performance is to find *balance* in every facet of your approach to leadership.

As a leader, you will always be faced with pressing issues, regardless of the endeavor. However, if you seek a balanced approach regarding these challenges, you will strengthen your attempts to produce a more desirable and predictable outcome.

The balanced approach and good common sense are synonymous in that both require constant examination of every aspect of your leadership principles, soup to nuts! This is a continuous process that doesn't end once you have achieved a position or title.

The preferred method regarding a good, balanced approach is to align all leadership traits and practices to the center, not too far to the left and not too far to the right, keeping every aspect of your leadership skills in perfect balance.

As humans, there will always be challenges and temptations in life that have the ability to get us off course. You may be equipped to recover from many life-changing events while others may prove detrimental both personally and professionally; no one is impervious or immune to life challenges and developments. We all will face some sort of evolution in life, but how we deal with the events as they unfold will ultimately determine our future.

I have an associate who told me a story regarding a company he once worked for in California. I will not mention any names due to the sensitive nature of this discussion.

There was a gentleman whom he knew very well who climbed the corporate ladder within his organization. He went on to explain how this gentleman worked hard and finally achieved an executive position and was transferred to a different state. One day, there was a breaking-news story regarding this young man. An unfortunate event had occurred: he had committed suicide.

A very tragic end to a promising individual, he explained. As we continued our discussion, I wondered out loud, "What could have gotten so far out of balance in his life to cause him to go this extreme and make this final decision?" As we concluded the discussion, we both surmised that we might never know.

This real-life situation was very impactful to the lives of many left behind by the choice this individual made. This illustrates what can happen if you don't pursue a balanced approach to life.

Having a balanced life is a healthy common sense endeavor from a personal and professional perspective. As mentioned, life is full of challenges; there is no denying this fact. However, when life challenges happen to bring you to a crossroad and you end up going down the wrong path, it doesn't mean that you can't find your way and get back on course.

Having a balanced life has the ability to help produce a more fruitful outcome when faced with life challenges and temptations. To further examine the importance of the balance principle, let's take a look at a couple of widely known events that were impactful and damaging to the lives of many:

In religion, many church leaders begin their journey by partaking in a noble and worthy cause. The initial goal is to learn about the importance of having a spiritual connection with God and how to live an orderly life in accordance with theology.

Christianity is indeed very important to the millions who attend church regularly or who hold a position in a house of worship. As a nation, the ethos regarding spiritual values is so ingrained and such a source of strength that the words "In God We Trust" is printed on our currency.

Nonetheless, history has taught us that even church leaders are not infallible, particularly when they attempt to operate above spiritual law. When a church leader engages in self-serving narcissistic behavior, it does nothing more than lead themselves and their followers down a path of destruction. The Jim Jones and David Koresh stories are prime examples that illustrate what can happen when you lose your balance.

In politics, many government officials start their careers from humble beginnings. Their parents may have been politicians or public servants, and their desire to serve the general public became the hallmark of their own careers. Like church leaders, the purpose of political service is truly a great endeavor—what better way of giving back to the community or the world at large than to serve people?

However, the spotlight has a way of blinding many people. They become disillusioned by the position; power and greed begins to take its unshakable hold until many believe that they can operate above the law. Typically, this is when the downward spiral begins to take form, and without question, you know the end result; the stories of former member of Congress Jesse Jackson Jr. and former Illinois Governor Rod Blagojevich are again a prime example of what can happen when you lose your balance.

In both scenarios, these leaders undoubtedly had some level of great potential; however, their ability, or lack thereof, to use good common sense regarding their chosen endeavors became their downfall. They lost their balance and fell from that tightrope we call life. In addition, with one stroke, the lives of those left behind to deal with the aftermath were sorely impacted.

Regardless of the endeavor, regardless of the challenge, finding balance in life should always be one of your greatest quests. For work, school, home, family, church, and even play, the goal should be to strike a perfect balance to ensure that you keep your footing and keep every aspect of life on course.

Undoubtedly, mistakes will be made along the voyage; you haven't lived until you have experienced some of life's challenges. Situations will always change us; it's a fact of life that we can't deny. However, mistakes and situations are there to help us grow, enriching our lives and helping us reach our full potential (depending on how we react to the developments). With growth comes experience, and with experience comes knowledge. With knowledge comes common sense, and with common sense comes wisdom—a desired state of mind that will give way to a balanced lifestyle.

I have a replica of a scale on my desk; because it's a replica, it's perfectly balanced. Whenever I look at this scale, it serves as a reminder of how life should be—*balanced*—both personally and professionally. Throughout life, I've learned that challenges will always come; difficulties will undoubtedly challenge our mental capacity. However, I firmly believe that finding your balance is unequivocally one of the most transitional and rewarding endeavors in life.

A balanced approach to life is very rewarding; it helps you to deal with stressful situations or those life-changing events that have the ability to tip the scale in a precarious direction and can help you surmount nearly every obstacle, both personally and professionally.

V

The Existence Principle

In the world of business, there have been many once-great organizations that no longer exist. They once fulfilled a need and occupied a space and time, but leadership failures ultimately caused their demise. There are hundreds of organizations that fall in this category. Here is a short list that is quite impressive: Wang Laboratories, the Rath Packing Company, Enron, and WorldCom, just to name a few. In their heyday, these firms were indeed giants in their respective industries. However, those appropriately mentioned "invisible forces" helped silence these once-great organizations.

It is undeniable that good commonsense leadership plays an essential role in the success and longevity of any organization. If you were to examine any of the aforementioned firms, you could point to egregious leadership failures at some point during their existence. Conversely, some will say that more firms fail from "top-down" leadership failures. This statement is very true from a broad perspective, particularly as it relates to the aforementioned firms that no longer exist. However, an organization can fail from the "bottom-up" as well. Case in point, read on:

Let's say that you operate a business in a market in which the labor pool is a little tight. You have a good distribution network to supply your company with all of the raw materials necessary to continue operations for years on end. This is a good thing; however, if you experience too many labor-related issues that dissatisfy your work-group, you may end up experiencing a decline in production or an inability to meet consumer demand. These types of situations will ultimately drive you out of business or force you to relocate your organization.

It is important for leaders to understand and cherish the contributions employees make because they are in fact "contributors" (which we will briefly explore in the next chapter). They aptly supply the physical labor necessary that fuels the organization. Just as a manufacturer needs raw materials to produce a particular product from a supplier, you will need labor to supply the skills necessary to produce a particular product or provide a particular service.

Employees are the key component to the overall success of any firm. If your goal is to have an organization that is built to last and withstand the test of time, every person under the proverbial umbrella of the organization must be fully committed to the success of the organization.

That said, it is extremely important for leaders to create a strong organizational culture that breathes life into the firm. The culture of an organization should be one where no employee, regardless of rank or level within the organization, takes a backseat and where employees' thoughts and ideas are embraced. Your organization should be a place where employees feel a sense of worth and take immense pride in their positions. It should be a place where employees feel proud to be part of a team and will go that extra mile to complete tasks and assignments. Let's examine this concept at work:

Say that you are the owner of a popcorn company with branches throughout the United States, offering a wide variety of flavors to tickle the palate. You have been very successful at creating a culture within your organization. You have an open-door policy for every store manager and promote autonomy throughout every outlet. Your employees love their individual customer base. People from all walks of life come to your shops daily just to purchase a bag or tin container of your delicious popcorn.

One day, a local news reporter decided to run a story on the success of your company. The reporter asked to interview several employees while they were serving customers to present a real-life setting for the network audience. While employees were serving customers, the reporter couldn't help but notice that everyone appeared to be very happy in their roles as they proudly provided great service with a smile to every customer who walked through the door.

As the reporter began to interview several team members, he said, "You all appear to be extremely happy in your roles. How do you stay so upbeat with the mad rush of customers and lines outside the door?" The team leader turns to the reporter and passionately stated, "We bleed popcorn! This is the reason we work here!"

Now that's pretty hardcore to bleed popcorn or virtually impossible, right? However, the point here is that this is the type of work environment great leaders create, one that makes the seemingly impossible, possible, and what is meant by creating a culture that thrives within an organization.

When leadership applies measured focus on the culture that resides within the organization, it will essentially create an environment in which all employees feel a part of something much larger than themselves. Creating an organizational culture has the ability to produce a level of energy unmatched by the competition, regardless of the industry. Moreover, creating organizational culture will provide fertile ground for an unwavering commitment and passion to the overall success of the organization. Therefore, the goal should be to inject culture into the organization and to avoid making it simply a place to work.

Conversely, before you can inject culture, you must first identify what's most important to your employees. You will need to check the heart of the organization because otherwise it is not possible to determine the direction of the organization from the employee perspective.

For years, many firms have used independent studies to gauge employee satisfaction in the workplace. Programs such as Annual Employee Engagement, Survey Action Feedback, and Employee 360 Feedback are some of the more popular studies in business. These studies have the ability to check the pulse of the organization; however, they are not very effective at getting to the heart of what matters most to employees.

The ability to lead groups or teams essentially involves a commonsense approach that requires leaders to dig a litter deeper to get to the root of what truly satisfies employees. There is a wonderful article by writer Issie Lapowsky titled "10 Things Employees Want Most." This is a must-read article for anyone currently in or aspiring to a leadership role.

According to Lapowsky's research, the following "wants" are considered most important to employees:

1. Employees want purpose—people want the chance to make a difference.
2. Employees want goals—those that are measurable and obtainable.
3. Employees want responsibility—they crave your trust.
4. Employees want autonomy—let people figure out the best path to achieve a goal.
5. Employees want flexibility—give consideration to their personal and professional lives.

6. Employees want attention—take time to look them in the eye and ask how they are doing.
7. Employees want opportunities for innovation—encourage employees to work on innovative ideas and allow them time for it.
8. Employees want open-mindedness—treat employees as equal partners when they come to you with fresh ideas.
9. Employees want transparency—they need to be aware of the direction of the organization.
10. Employees want compensation—pay people enough to take the discussion surrounding money off the table by way of salaries, bonuses, and benefits.

Each point in Lapowsky's article provides more detailed discussion regarding employee issues in today's workplace. What I find most salient is that each requires a good commonsense approach to achieve a desired level of success.

This article also highlights the deployment strategy of Meddius, a software company based, in Charlottesville, Virginia. Meddius utilized many of these principles to achieve a greater level of success for the organization and its employees.

One side note regarding Lapowsky's article: Compensation was not the most important thing valued by employees. Compensation is very important to all employees but not the number-one source of job fulfilment. Food for thought!

VI

The Employee-Contributor Principle

Many modern business educators and leaders suggest that one of the most important assets of a firm is its employees. Some would argue that they are not, and some would say that they are just employees. After all is said and done, I submit to you that employees are *contributors* as they relate to the success of the organization, its shareholders, and its other stakeholders. These trifectas are the true benefactors of the employees who work diligently, day and night, and are committed to their craft and overall success of the organization.

Webster's New World Dictionary defines "contribute" as follows:

1. To give jointly with others
2. To write an article
3. To furnish ideas

Steven C. Duncan

I find definitions one and three to be rather profound in that:

1. Most employees typically work together (jointly) toward the common good of the organization.
2. Many employees do in fact furnish ideas to improve the working environment, for example, suggestion box or bright-idea programs.

The definition offered by *Webster*'s helps bring into focus the term *contributor* because assets are things a firm owns, such as vehicles, equipment, or buildings. Employees are defined as persons who work for wages. Neither of these traditional definitions fit with the definition for *contribute* simply because employees are not assets and most employees do not merely work for a wage.

The people element is the most important dimension of any organization. Even if an organization claims to be fully automated, human intervention is still required simply because machines will break down, computers will malfunction, and robots will require regular maintenance. Therefore, the importance of the people element in any organization can't be denied.

Assuredly, employees are the lifeblood of any organization; no firm can adequately exist without them.

VII

The Seek-and-Find Principle

Another great benefit of a good commonsense approach helps leaders recognize that those individuals who report to work daily to perform their task and assignments aren't just merely employees, quite the contrary. The best commonsense leaders will deploy a strategy to actively search for the next generation of leaders within the organization and assist those who aspire to a leadership role.

For leaders who fall into this category, it could be said that there is no uneasiness or narcissism when searching for potential leaders. These leaders are typically very comfortable in their own skin and will not hesitate to reach across the aisle in search of the next up-and-coming leaders.

Moreover, good commonsense leaders possess a firm understanding that, sooner or later, the next generation of leaders will come. Therefore, they take an active role in developing aspiring leaders. When good common sense prevails in these situations, the organization, shareholders, and stakeholders benefit immensely.

The contributions of frontline employees are endless—from McDonald's to Burger King, from Kroger supermarket to Walmart—thousands of employees support the organizations in ways that many leaders within the firms simply can't do on their own.

Now there are in fact different levels of contributors. Some are very happy making daily contributions at a level suitable for their talent. Typically, these employees are very good and efficient at performing their daily task. It may be a forklift driver working in a warehouse, an individual working in the customer-service department at the local grocery store, a teller working at a local bank, or a cook preparing meals at the corner restaurant.

What's important here is to recognize and engage those individuals who aspire to growth, development, and opportunity within their place of work. Perhaps the best forklift driver desires to become the next forklift trainer, perhaps the employee who is an excellent customer-service representative desires to become the next department manager, perhaps the employee who is the best teller ever desires to becomes the next head teller, or perhaps the cook preparing meals at the corner restaurant desires to become a restaurant manager or owner.

It is undeniable that the longevity of any organization depends greatly on the current and future level of employee engagement by corporate leadership. In today's competitive work environment, the development of future leaders is an ever-present and pressing issue. If you are currently in a leadership role, it should be considered an honor and privilege to be in a position to help shape and influence the path for the next generation of leaders, but more importantly, accept it as your responsibility! By doing so, you'll help set the tone for the overall longevity and success of the organization that you may be passionately a part of. Frankly, you may also find this endeavor to be one that is very fruitful and personally rewarding. I have found that the engagement of grooming future leaders has helped me to identify with their goals and aspirations, thus leading to a more positive growth strategy for those whom I served, including myself. In short, as they grow, so do you!

To know that you have performed outside the normal scope of your duties and responsibilities to assist others' professional growth and development as future leaders is truly gratifying. In truth, it's a way of giving back, not only to the organization but to the betterment of society as well.

The best commonsense approach regarding this principle and leadership is to "inspire those who aspire." Leaders who engage in this approach understand that their ultimate success in not based solely on their individual performance but on the performance of those whom they serve. In short, they understand that it takes the sum of the parts to make a whole. They never undermine or downplay the contributions the employee makes. Moreover, they seek input from those individuals who so richly influence the success of the organization.

The point here is that regardless of the level of leadership or status within the organization, good commonsense leaders realize that the contributions employees make each and every day are immense and very important to the success of the organization.

Now there is one segment that in nearly every organization gets little attention but requires mentioning: the decision-making process. When important decisions that impact employees are made, management will typically assemble a team of managers or other decision-makers, not those who will be impacted the most, the employees. Why is this so? There could be several explanations: fear of relinquishing control to subordinates (the-inmates-running-the-asylum syndrome), lack of trust and confidence, the desire to have the light shine on oneself, or even one's own insecurities.

These reasons along with many others are damaging and underscore a weakness that can hinder the overall success of any organization. Granted, there are confidential and sensitive matters that should be handled accordingly; however, whenever there is an opportunity to involve employees in the decision-making process, leaders should not hesitate to engage them in the process. The byproduct is an environment in which people feel a part of the process, a greater feeling of worth and purpose to the organization, and a place where creativity and energy flows freely.

Steven C. Duncan

It is quite possible to shortchange your leadership potential by not seeking your employees' input when making important decisions regarding their work environment. Those who perform daily tasks and assignments are the ones who know best, and the information they provide could prove valuable and impactful to the end results. Good commonsense leaders are fully aware of the value employees bring to the table and never underestimate the fundamentals of developing healthy manager-employee relationships.

As an extension, there are social ramifications when employees are excited and feel good about their place of work; it has the tendency to carry over into their personal lives. Interaction with neighbors, friends, and family tend to be more fruitful and enjoyable. Conversely, bad days at work can have a negative impact and will typically spill over into personal life, if an individual cannot unplug from the events of the day.

When I was a young lad, the family could tell when dad had a bad day at work. The best approach would be to stay out of his way, go to your room, read a book, or listen to the stereo. Mom and my other siblings were pretty good at managing dad's bad days, which were in fact few. However, other families in the neighborhood where I grew up were not so fortunate at times.

Now the purpose here is not to suggest that leaders within an organization are responsible for their employees' actions outside the work environment, but make no mistake:

In today's competitive work environment, there is a thin line between home life and work life. In truth, when you calculate the amount of time spent at work, including the commute, it's easy to surmise that work life can be impactful and influential on an individual's private life.

Good commonsense leaders understand the social-responsibility angle as it relates to work and personal life. They understand that there must be a balance between the two parts and the direct influence one could possibly have on the other. This may not be the main focus of most leaders, but it's important to note how your interaction with your subordinates can determine the direction of the organization and community at large. Therefore, *seek* out those issues that are most important to your team, involve them as much as possible in the decision-making process, and you will *find* that you've created an environment that is more fertile and rich with new ideas and energy that will not only benefit the organization but also society as well.

VIII

The Visionary Principle

In every firm, you can find "diamonds-in-the-rough" employees; like natural diamonds, they are very rare. They are often those who are unseen or barely noticed. They quietly go about performing their daily task but quite possibly possess the skills and talents necessary to take the firm or organization to the next level.

When we examine the origin of natural diamonds, we find that they are formed from a carbon substance, typically deep beneath the earth's surface, that is subject to intense heat and pressure over a long period of time. When excavated from the earth's surface, natural diamonds are full of imperfections. It takes an artisan, one who is skilled and experienced, to take a diamond that is totally imperfect and turn it into a beautiful gemstone. If you are in a leadership role, I submit to you that you are that artisan!

Now the greater question is who are these exceptional individuals, these so-called rough gemstones? Are they those individuals who sit on the board of directors, the members of executive management, or project management? Perhaps, but there is one group of individuals who cannot be overlooked—the group that works directly for you, your employees. It's those individuals who perform daily tasks and assignments necessary to ensure the success of the organization. It's those individuals who can prove to be the most valuable to your organization.

More often than not, that diamond-in-the-rough type of employee possesses characteristics that help fuel organizational success. His or her work parallels a commitment to the success of the organization. Their approach to work is unwavering, and they are in fact creative problem solvers. He or she doesn't give way to narcissistic behaviors, and possesses a firm understanding of the core principles of respect for others. Moreover, they possess a fervent can-do attitude and is typically the one you can count on when you need that extra effort most.

Now it is possible to have many individuals who fall within this category but, again, the goal is to adroitly search for that diamond, the standout, the champion, who aspires to contribute at a different level.

The big vision for any firm is not confined to executive management or the board of directors. In fact, many ideas to improve operational performance come directly from the employees. These individuals can be the difference makers between being a **good organization** and becoming a **great organization**. To elaborate, let's look at the difference between the two:

Good organizations exist throughout the marketplace. These are firms that have found their niche and are usually very good at what they do. Typically, decisions are made by the upper management—the skybox effect, or in a vacuum, if you will. Employees are not included in the decision-making process or at best, a minimal attempt to tap into the employee knowledge base is made. In these firms, employees are reminded to "just do your job" and/or reminded that "this is what you are paid to do," thus leaving the employee feeling devalued or less appreciated as it relates to their thoughts and ideas regarding their place of employment. Moreover, firms that fall in this category will essentially experience a higher level of turnover. Thus, the end result is lost productivity, lower production, and a less-than-motivated workforce.

Great organizations possess a fervent understanding of their employee knowledge base. Leadership in these firms typically creates a culture of inclusion and is disciplined in its efforts to ensure that employees are involved in the decision-making process at nearly every level. In these firms, creative minds are not restricted; they're embraced. In this transitional environment, employees are encouraged to set aside self-serving behaviors that can be detrimental or impactful with regard to the success of the organization.

Essentially, employees and management are encouraged to be unified in their quest to achieve common goals for the overall betterment of the organization. These firms understand that it is shortsighted to not include employees' thoughts and ideas regarding productivity and production in the workplace. They understand that the person who performs the job each and every day possesses a keen understanding of what it takes to improve job performance. Lastly, in these firms, that old US Navy slogan rings true: "It's not just a job; it's an adventure," one that can take you many places within the organization.

There are countless stories of individuals who started working in the mailroom, bused tables, or swept floors and later became one of the firm's top executives or CEO. This is not some strange phenomenon for great organizations—quite the contrary, it's by design. One can point to the culture that resides within the organization that makes it possible. In addition, it illustrates what can happen when employees are truly involved in the overall success of an organization.

As mentioned in previous chapters, a good commonsense approach for leadership in any firm should always be to reach beyond the obvious. Leaders should always take a first and second look at their employees, spend quality time with them, and solicit their thoughts and ideas regarding the business. By doing so, leaders will find that many of the best and brightest ideas are not always found at the executive level or in the boardroom. You should never underestimate the knowledge your employees can bring to the table.

For many years, I worked for what is today one of our nation's largest public firms, Federal Express. After three years in the courier ranks, I was promoted to the level of management. Shortly thereafter, I was enrolled in a mandatory twelve-week managerial training program.

During one of our daily training sessions, I recall when one of our lead instructors (who was a corporate vice president) was conducting one of his great presentations regarding leadership. He passionately stated, "When faced with a dilemma, always get someone in the boat with you because it is easier to row upstream with others paddling with you rather than going it alone." As an eager yet novice manager, I quickly raised my hand to assert that my peers and superiors would be the individuals in the boat with me, correct? However, to my surprise, this was not the case. In his rebuttal, the vice president explained that peers and superiors are in fact important in this scenario, but more importantly, you cannot abandon your employees' thoughts and/or ideas in the problem-solving process because, in most cases, they already have the answers!

This level of thinking by upper management has undoubtedly contributed to the success FedEx enjoys today. Moreover, this statement taught me a valuable lesson regarding good commonsense leadership and the importance of the employee element to the organization. Some twenty-eight years later, this is still one of the hallmarks of my leadership traits as I have learned to value employees' thoughts and ideas.

Throughout the years, I have worked with many individuals who aspired to leadership roles and assisted them in achieving their dreams within various organizations. Not for notoriety or egotistical motives, but because it was the right thing to do for the organization and the betterment of those whom I served.

I learned to look past criticism and hearsay of individual employees from their peers, and often superiors, in search of that "diamond-in-the-rough" type of employee. I have been very successful by taking this approach simply because I've learned to look for good leadership traits in those aspiring to develop their careers and not heed the personal innuendos made against an individual.

Conversely, most leaders will typically look to promote those who they are most comfortable with. Those who are in their inner circle—family members, friends of friends, long-time associates, etc.—get promoted. Good commonsense leaders will look to break that circle to form a straight line so that they are better able to reach individuals who do not lie within that proverbial inner circle. Doing so helps leaders see beyond what appears to be the obvious and tap into talent that could not be realized as long as they continued to operate within that circle.

Reaching beyond the obvious is relative in terms of finding that previously mentioned "diamond-in-the-rough" type of individual. Here is a case in point:

In the year two-thousand, Tom Brady, a college football quarterback who played for Michigan, was a *sixth*-round draft choice of the New England Patriots. If you're a fan of football, then you already know the story: four Super Bowl championships, three-time Super Bowl MVP, countless honors, a future Hall of Fame candidate; need I say more?!

Whether you're a tenured or novice leader, it is important to understand how to use your skills and abilities acquired to become an effective leader today helps to shape the future for the next generation of leaders to come. This is something that all leaders must be keenly cognizant of if we are to remain competitive and a leader in the global arena. Therefore, it's important that we share good commonsense practices and principles simply because what we do today as leaders will ultimately impact the future for tomorrow's great leaders.

In my opinion, the aforesaid is the best commonsense approach as it relates to finding visionaries within any organization. Again, it's these individuals who are often overlooked but may possess the skills, talents, and abilities that can quite possibly propel your organization to the next level.

IX

The R-E-S-P-E-C-T Principle

For those young enough to remember, the song "R-E-S-P-E-C-T" by R&B singer Aretha Franklin was a number-one hit on the pop charts in 1967, earning her two Grammy Awards in 1968—a great song indeed. However, the focus of this discussion is not the song or lyrics; it's the word in and of itself.

Respect is a principle that is often forgotten by many in leadership roles. Leaders in both business and political arenas are guilty of this truth. Today, this is one of the reasons why we find so many leaders facing ethical dilemmas. In business, we find leaders who are demoted and some who even get fired for poor ethics, for intimidation, or for sexual harassment. In politics, we witness Congress with an approval rating at single-digit levels because elected officials simply can't work together on the issues facing our nation or they have personal agendas. The ability to abide by legal and ethical requirements is an important element as it relates to the respect principle.

Those who are in positions of influence, regardless of the level of experience, and who have arrived at an aspired level in their career should not discard the respect principle. Quite the contrary, this should be the one trait that you latch onto and zealously guard because the consequences could prove damaging both personally and professionally.

Good commonsense leaders realize that respect for others is one of the single most important leadership attributes they can ever possess. They understand that respect for others is not merely an affectation but that it has the ability to move to the heart of what matters most to those whom they serve. They understand that respect for others is not a facade nor does it have to be excessive. It only needs to be genuine.

Additionally, commonsense leaders understand how this trait applies from a personal perspective as well; self-respect is equally important as respect for others. Continual self-examination is an ongoing commonsense practice for leaders, be it personal or professional. They understand that the quest for excellence greatly depends on what they say and do. They understand that this attribute is an important factor of remaining above reproach in all business dealings. They understand that the "person is more important than the seat." You never want to find yourself in a position of derision in which people respect your position in an organization but not you as a leader—authority and leadership are not synonymous. They also steer clear from narcissistic behavior that can prove detrimental to their career.

Respect is truly an all-encompassing principle. It's important to the receiver as well as the user, and there are mutual benefits when properly applied. Another case in point:

I was watching a network program about prisoners inside a state penitentiary. One of the corrections officers who was being interviewed was discussing one particular aspect that was most important to prisoners—respect. For individuals who are incarcerated, many feel that respect is the only thing that they have left.

The corrections officer went on to explain how information is often exchanged behind prison walls, adding that when you treat prisoners with respect, you'd be surprised by the information they provide you!

I found this corrections officer's engagement with inmates profound in that he was able to apply the respect principle to gather information about what goes on behind prison walls, gain access to information known only to a few selected inmates, and help rid the system of corruption.

The assumption is that a common good resulted from this officer's effort and a mutual benefit was achieved. Typically, the final outcome of these types of interviews is not divulged for the safety and security of the prisoners and officers; however, there is one thing that we can surmise: If a corrections officer figured out how to get the most from inmates simply by treating them with respect and dignity, imagine the possibilities when leaders deploy the same strategy outside prison walls?

Respect is truly a learned behavior, not an inborn trait. To elaborate, commonsense disciplines are typically acquired at an early age by those who bring us into the world and who care for us at a time when we don't really know ourselves. As our lives start to take shape and as we begin to interact with society, we are taught the core values of self-respect and respect for others. It becomes part of our DNA and a redolent discipline regarding the way we interact with each other as humans. In retrospect, those who nurture us until we become adults understand the extrinsic and intrinsic values of respect. We were constantly reminded of this discipline at home, school, work, and even at competitive play until it became a part of our identity.

You can never underestimate the power of respect; it's truly a key attribute that follows us through the chapters of our life. Conversely, respect is so powerful that it has the ability to transition common sense to the realms of wisdom—a result that should be our greatest quest.

Essentially, the respect principle has the ability to help get you where you want to be, and it can take you where you want to go, both personally and professionally. It's a characteristic that comes with great responsibility but the load it brings is not very heavy. In truth, it's virtually weightless when good common sense is applied.

To elaborate on the latter statement, respect (both self-respect and respect for others) is a transitional trait and is typically a reflection of a person's upbringing. Basically, it's a reflection of how we were raised at a young age and how we were able to cope with adversity and challenges while transitioning to adulthood. For example, while growing up on the South Side of Chicago, we played slow-pitch softball during the summer months at the stadium near where we lived. The group of players from my block would typically play a team from the neighboring block in a competitive game of softball to determine which neighborhood had the best overall team. We would flip a coin to determine which team would bat first and from there, the game was on!

Older adults who lived in the neighborhood would often come out and watch us play. They would cheer for both teams when a great play was made or when someone cracked a home run over the fence. At the end of each game, win or lose, we would walk over to the opposing team, shake hands, and congratulate each other on a good game.

A simple analogy, but the point here is that as we played hard to win, we always showed a level of respect for our opponents and each other as a team. If we won, we celebrated; if we lost, we still celebrated. Even the adults who sat in the stands watching the game would cheer for both teams. They had no favorite; they just enjoyed watching us play, regardless of the outcome. At the time, little did we know that the adults sitting in the stands were teaching us that winning wasn't the most important thing—the respect we had for our fellow players was.

Respect is a trait not given simply because of title or position, money, or power; respect is undoubtedly an earned and learned behavior. It's a trait that can take a lifetime to build but that can be lost in a matter of seconds.

As previously mentioned, respect is truly a relatively simple trait that involves a good commonsense approach. It is relative not only to ourselves but also, more importantly, to how we interact with others. Now there will always be things in life that will challenge our mental capacity or transition our thought process to areas different from what we were taught as children; however, respect we have for ourselves and each other as humans, is the one trait we should never let escape us—it's truly a road that runs both ways.

X

The Positive Principle

Of all the things we experience in life, the one thing I find most fascinating is how people are drawn to negative aspects of life. Be it an event, a situation, or some other development, people are captivated by the sensationalism of negativity and give little regard to the positive aspects of life from both a personal and professional perspective. To elaborate, let's take a look at the following situation:

Let's say that you are a proud homeowner who has a 100 percent track record of paying the monthly bills on time for the last ten years. One week you are out of town on business or pleasure (your choice), and when you return home, you go to the mailbox and retrieve the mail as usual. As you open your mail, you discover that you missed the mortgage payment for the month and now you're hit with a late fee (depending on your mortgage company).

Eyes wide, you realize the magnitude of the situation and hurry to the phone and call the mortgage company. You get a representative on the line and apologize for being late, explain that it was an honest mistake, and accept full responsibility. After you finish pleading your case, the representative advises that there is nothing that can be done; you must pay the late charges and it will count against your credit score…ouch!

Now bad things happen to good people all the time—to be human is to sometimes err; however, situations like the one just described deserve special consideration or at least one would think so! Now it's one thing if a person is late every month. Then our discussion would be quite different. But in this case, there should be a more commonsense approach to help the consumer who made an honest mistake.

Perhaps a case could be made by the consumer with his or her mortgage company due to a strong on-time payment history. The real point of all of this is that there is very little consideration for all of the positive things we do or adhere to each and every day. It's the negative events that typically get the most attention, even if they are as minor as a tempest in a teapot.

In today's fast-paced, competitive world, information flows rapidly. It comes at us so fast that we have little time to consider all the good that people do. Let one bad thing happen, however, and watch where all of the attention is directed. In truth, our world is dominated by negativity.

Steven C. Duncan

We get bombarded daily with negative local or national news reports. Crime and politics seem to dominate the headlines. Speaking of the latter, our political landscape, particularly during an election cycle, is filled with so much mudslinging, backbiting, and divisive tactics; it's enough to keep your head spinning—all in an attempt to vilify the opponent's reputation or gain the upper hand to sway voters. Nonetheless, we are drawn to this behavior like a magnet to steel.

There is a psychological aspect to negative thinking. After conducting a little Internet research on this topic, I've determined that you could write a five-hundred-page document covering this subject. However, for the sake of discussion, we'll stick to a more simplified version. To understand this phenomenon, we must first understand why we are so drawn to its effects.

Negativity is a learned behavior; we are not born into this world with negative thoughts or negative ideas about this place we call earth. Besides their adorability, children are completely innocent and oblivious to the complexities of our world. This could explain the reason why our little ones are loved so deeply; they have not been influenced or tainted by society.

As children reach puberty, they begin to process those things that surround them and assimilate what they have learned. They begin to listen to their parents and friends; they begin to watch and/or listen to media outlets, and they start to form their own ideas about life and society as a whole. By the time they reach adulthood, the level of exposure to those negative aspects of life has captured their imagination and has engulfed their everyday life.

This is no strange phenomenon; this is simply our world as we know it. Now what level of impact can be surmised from this analogy? Your guess is as good as mine, but should you have any doubts about the impact of negativity, may I suggest that you lean forward and take a look around.

Needless to say, one burning question still remains: How can we overcome these unenthusiastic attitudes that so dominate our daily lives? The answer lies in the use of good common sense.

From the outset of the discussion of this principle, I reviewed some of the salient issues that exist in our daily lives. Looking back, let me introduce several "perhaps" scenarios to help us better understand the benefits of invoking commonsense practices:

In the world of politics, political combatants jockey for position to win their party's nomination or seat at the city, state, or federal level. Typically, these events will bring out the "best of the worst" in the individual candidates and supporters. As mentioned earlier, this is when we witness an array of follies in an attempt to foil an opponent's opportunity. The insatiable desire to smear an individual's reputation is driven only by the eagerness to win and beat the competition at any cost! From personal attacks regarding individual character and integrity to bathroom jokes, if you will, negativity is the common theme in most campaigns.

Steven C. Duncan

Unequivocally, competitiveness is the nature of politics and from a personal perspective, I find that it's okay to "agree to disagree" at times, but *perhaps* it's better to focus on healthy discussions surrounding the issues instead of hurling insults or using divisive tactics. Any individual with political ambitions should understand that deleterious behavior truly undermines the purpose and intent of our political system. Also, debates should reflect a healthy and substantive assessment of the positions of the candidates. To stand out from the crowd, you must operate above the fray and focus on the issues at hand.

In the age of mass media, there are enormous amounts of money spent to "cover the story," many of which are marred by negative highlights that are fashionably called "breaking news" or "breaking report." I find this very interesting but true. Take a look at a case in point:

During a recent business trip, my flight was delayed. While waiting for the next available flight, a "breaking-news" story flashed across the television screen. The story was in fact a tragic event involving death and destruction. As I stood watching the report with eyes glued and heart pounding, I couldn't help but notice the number of other people gathering to watch the same report with eyes glued (and heart pounding, I assume). As I walked away from the gathering throng, I pondered whether a "breaking-news" report would receive the same attention if the story line read "Humanitarian efforts help save lives in Somalia" or "Breakthrough research has promising developments in the quest to cure cancer" or "Patient receives a successful liver transplant."

Media outlets are predominantly filled with negative reporting; this is the reason why so many people don't watch the news. I've heard many people say, "I really don't watch the news because it's too depressing." I assume that you've heard this at some point in time or perhaps have the same position. Networks such as MSNBC, FOX, and CNN consume our day, hours on end, with reports of tragedy, political upheaval, and mayhem. Negative reporting tickles the psychological dimension we have been exposed to the majority of our adult lives—so to reiterate, negativity is a "learned" behavior.

Now the purpose of this passage is not meant to undermine the importance of how networks report the news. In fact, some negative reporting is good because it has the ability to heighten our awareness of events that can impact our daily lives. But *perhaps* a better commonsense approach would be to blend positive human-interest stories (not just a two- or three-minute segment) with other daily news reports.

Quite frankly, positive news reporting can be just as impactful as negative news reports that saturate our daily lives. Just as there are enough bad things in this world to report, there are just as many good things for viewers to enjoy as well!

In the world of business, leaders face the daily challenge of meeting production quotas or getting the job done within an allocated amount of time. As a tenured member of management, I certainly attest to the many challenges of getting the job done in a timely and productive fashion.

I also understand that not every employee will possess the bandwidth to meet production or productivity goals. This is especially true for newer employees or those who have transferred into a new role because there are learning curves in any new position. Some employees may grasp the mechanics of the position quickly and be solid contributors from the outset, while others may take what appears to be an eternity.

Typically, this is when your leadership skills are tested; the production quotas haven't changed, the standards haven't changed, the metrics haven't changed, and so the pressure is on to get everybody up to speed and quickly!

This is pretty common in most businesses, right? However, you may have an employee doing his or her level best but not well enough to meet the operational standards. Now it's fairly easy to document employee performance (particularly trends) and communicate to the employee that there is a problem or issue various levels of discipline in an attempt to adjust the employee's performance. But a good commonsense approach is to take the road less traveled, move away from assumptions, and get to the root of the problem, first!

Individual consideration is another very important leadership trait in the world of business. The ability of leaders to dig a little deeper and gain insight into individual employee-performance barriers is essential to improving work performance.

I submit to you that employees don't get out of bed every morning, shower, get dressed, and spend time commuting to work daily just to do a poor job! It just doesn't compute. *Perhaps* the issues may be systemic in nature and totally out of the employee's control; *perhaps* it may be an Illness or physical limitation that's impacting performance, or *perhaps* it may be personal in nature—for example, a death in the family, the failing health of a loved one, having to care for a sick child or parent after work, etc.

The point here is to drill down to the issues that are impacting performance and develop a strategy (with the employee) to achieve a desired result, one that is measurable and attainable.

Individual consideration is not some new-age leadership phenomenon; however, it is often forgotten in favor of meeting or exceeding organization goals. Now I would be remiss if I failed to mention that this method is not 100 percent foolproof. It may not work in every situation, but for the many years I have been a member of management, it is the most-trusted leadership trait I know that has the ability to produce real and positive results.

Bottom line: Work to create a win-win situation for both parties involved so that at the end of the day, as a leader, you'll know for certain that you have done your level best to assist your subordinates who need help the most.

The purpose of the positive principle is to simply highlight the benefits of a good commonsense approach and move beyond the negative aspects that have the ability to weaken our emotional psyche. Essentially, emotions are something that we own; they are unequivocally part of our DNA. We all possess a wide range of emotions—from happy to sad, anxious to angry—all can be influenced by a host of life-changing events. However, it's important to note that your emotional psyche can interfere and even overrule good commonsense practices and applications.

Now there are many different techniques to help better control our emotions and position our entire compass toward good commonsense practices:

> **Think before you react:** Change the narrative and move beyond any situation that has the ability to promote negative reactions.
>
> **Think proactively:** When you position your thought process to a proactive posture, you are less likely to be influenced or persuaded by outside factors and events that can distract you from good commonsense practices.
>
> **Avoid knee-jerk reactions:** It is a good thing to stop and think before making a decision. Reflection regarding any situation helps to produce more reasonable and positive results.
>
> **Get the facts:** Whenever possible, make it a common practice to gather as much information as you can prior to making a decision. You may not always be 100 percent correct in your assessment—we are

human—but conducting a little research will get you closer to the bull's-eye. If nothing else, it will broaden your understanding of the situation.

I once read a wonderful quotation from one of the most popular US gymnastics champions, Mary Lou Retton, who said, "Everybody has to try just a little bit harder, do just a little bit better, think just a little deeper, work just a little longer." This statement, in of itself, provides an insightful assessment of good commonsense practices and principles.

XI

The Thread Principle

There is a commonality among all humans; quite simply, when we roll out of bed, we don our morning wear—whatever it may be. After a good breakfast, and before we leave our residence, we wrap ourselves with undergarments (unless you enjoy going commando), socks, stockings, shirts, pants, suits, slacks, dresses, coats, jackets, etc. However, there is one important piece of material that keeps everything we wear looking great: the *threads* of the garments that hold everything we wear together make us comfortable and our appearance acceptable.

London-based, high-end luxury designer Alexander Amosu crafts one of the most expensive suits a man can purchase. At a cost of nearly $101,000, the suit has more than five thousand stitches of platinum and gold thread. This suit is simply a gem and will undoubtedly make you look and feel ten times its value. However, should those platinum or gold threads begin to unravel due to improper care, the suit becomes nothing more than a piece of material, a shell of what it once was.

Continuing with our theme, good commonsense leaders understand that every facet of their organization depends greatly on that common thread to hold it all together. They understand the perils of operating in a vacuum and steer clear of behavior that could be construed as narcissistic or self-serving as it relates to the overall success of the organization.

To further examine this principle, let's take a look at one of the oldest and largest organizations known around the world, the US Department of Defense. With approximately 3.2 million civilian and military personnel, the Department of Defense is our nation's largest employer. There are five main branches of our nation's defense network: army, marines, navy, air force, and coast guard. They operate as one cohesive unit, working in harmony to protect our nation and our allies abroad. Now, let's examine the supporting roles of each branch:

- The army's primary function is not only to defend the interests of the United States but also to serve a supporting role worldwide with specialized equipment and personnel.
- The marines' primary function consists of deploying strike forces to control shorelines and clear the way for navy and army personnel.

- The navy's primary function is to patrol the open seas and protect territorial waters with ocean-going vessels specially designed to carry aircraft, assault missiles, and combat personnel.
- The air force's primary role is to provide air power and weapons in support of soldiers on the ground.
- The coast guard's primary function is to provide law enforcement and rescue services in coastal waters.

As you can see, each branch of the armed forces has a common thread. Each branch depends greatly on the others, particularly during wartime, in a quest to achieve victory and keep our nation safe and secure.

Due to the sheer scope and size of this magnificent organization, there are often many challenges, both internal and external, that can tear the very fabric of the organization. Top Pentagon officials understand this and work hard to ensure that internal structure of the organization and morale remain strong. To aid in this process, many top officials meet with soldiers and battalion commanders stationed around the globe to discuss strategies and missions. During times of war, they will also visit soldiers in the field, even partaking in meals to show their admiration, confidence, trust, and support for the difficult missions the troops are asked to perform. These efforts irrefutably help to keep morale at a level necessary to complete a mission or reach a stated goal.

It's no small wonder why the US Department of Defense is regarded as one of the most elite and effective organizations in the world. There is an enormous amount of effort, time, and money spent to ensure that this organization remains the best this nation has to offer and the best this world has ever known. There is truly a commitment to excellence and a common thread that runs deep within this superb organization.

In the private sector, one could ask why these same techniques aren't very noticeable or found in the workplace as they relate to employee-employer relationships? Now there could undoubtedly be a number of reasons why—too busy, not enough time in the day, more pressing issues and responsibilities, the appetite of upper management is just not there, this firm is not a democracy, etc.

For leaders, if these or other reasons are prevalent in your place of business, perhaps a different approach is in order. Leadership at General Electric got it right by issuing this statement: "Excellence is not a spectator sport; everyone's involved." This statement, in and of itself, speaks volume for any firm *if* the desire is to enrich the lives of employees and improve the overall performance, longevity, and success of the organization.

In the must-read article by Issie Lapowsky, she emphasizes that employees want attention. It is not enough to meet with employees to discuss an annual performance review or to have a monthly meeting when you have the opportunity to discuss matters with your employees daily. It is not enough to issue podcasts when you have the opportunity to meet or conduct town-hall meetings with your employees in person. It is not enough to conduct office campaigns when you have hundreds or even thousands of employees within the organization looking to you for guidance, and it is not enough to offer a thank-you letter when a personal handshake is much more powerful.

Leaders should "lead to inspire, not aspire to lead." By doing so, you tear down those proverbial walls that sometimes exist between employees and management. Leading to inspire has the ability to improve the level of trust and confidence necessary to create a world-class atmosphere within the organization. In addition, it helps leaders dig deeper into the inner workings of the organization—a check of the pulse or a health assessment, if you will—to determine the state of the organization from the employee perspective.

In the world of politics, many politicians realize that the most effective campaigns are won at the grassroots level. For business leaders, you will never win a campaign sitting behind a desk. Therefore, leadership, top-down, should conduct its own campaign within the organization. Get out and visit the employees in your organization, conduct in-person town-hall meetings, shake a few hands, and build that rapport to ensure that those platinum and gold threads of that Alexander Amosu-style organization that you lead remain strong and vibrant.

I once read an interesting quotation by author Bob Moawad who so wisely said, "If you're too busy to help the people around you succeed, you're too busy." Any firm's success depends greatly on the level of success of those whom it employs. Investing quality time in those who help make your organization a success will do nothing less than make your firm the world-class organization you so desire and built to withstand the test of time.

XII

The Beginning Principle

In life, everything starts with a beginning. How we begin the journey of careers is an element that is often forgotten by many successful leaders once they have "arrived" at a position in their careers or place in life. Suddenly, those things that were once cherished and important to your growth and development become secondary. Good commonsense leaders should never abandon or disregard the lessons learned along the journey that led to their career success. Let's examine the following example to illustrate the importance of others to our journey in life.

Let's say you live in Los Angeles and have planned a road trip to visit family and friends who reside in New York City. You do your homework and plot the roads and highways that will get you there in the most efficient manner. You estimate that the trip will take approximately forty hours and 2,451 miles. So you pack enough food, water, and clothing for the long journey. You grab your credit card and additional cash, load up your vehicle, say a prayer, and set out for New York.

The Journey, Day One:
About six hundred miles down the road, your steering wheel starts to shake. After pulling over to a safe place along the highway, you discover that you have a flat tire. You open your trunk and reach for the donut spare only to find that it's low on air. While you are attempting to change the flat tire, a commuter spots you, stops, and asks if you need a hand. You explain to the stranger that your spare is low on air. The stranger then replies, "I have an air pump; let me get it out of my trunk." So the stranger retrieves the air pump, inflates your spare tire, and provides you with directions to the nearest tire-repair shop. You offer compensation but the stranger replies, "No thank you, it was my pleasure." You drive about ten miles and spot the tire-repair shop. You get the tire repaired and continue on your journey to the nearest hotel to get some rest.

The Journey, Day Two:
Up bright and early the next day, you drive another six hundred miles, enjoying the scenery along the way, when all of a sudden your check-engine light turns on. You're able to make it to the nearest repair shop so that an analysis of the engine

can be performed. Shortly thereafter, you're advised that your alternator is bad and needs to be replaced. You explain to the repair-shop manager that you're driving from Los Angeles to New York City. He replies, "You must be exhausted, so I'll do you this favor: I'll put you next in line and will replace your alternator so that you can be on your way." With a smile you reply, "Thanks a lot!" So the repairs are made, and the mechanic performs an additional safety inspection on your vehicle to ensure that there are no other mechanical issues. The shop manager sends you on your way with a friendly wave. You drive several miles before deciding to take a break and get some food and rest at a local hotel and start your journey early the next morning.

The Journey, Day Three:

After driving another six hundred miles coupled with some small breaks in-between, you decide that it's time to get some real rest before making the final leg of your journey and drive to the nearest hotel. You decide to grab a bite to eat at a restaurant across the street before checking in to your hotel. You strike up a conversation with the waiter and start to discuss your road trip. You discuss the miles that you've already driven and the events that have taken place along the journey thus far. The waiter replies, "Well, let's get you a good hot meal so that you can get some rest and start out fresh in the morning." The waiter delivers your order; you enjoy the great food and service and are now ready to pay for the delicious meal. When you ask the waiter for the check, you discover that your meal has been paid for. You look startled for a moment and then ask the waiter, "How can this be? I haven't paid for my dinner." The waiter then explains that there was an older couple sitting behind you who overheard your conversation and decided to pay for your dinner in full, and even included the tip. In your amazement, you turn to thank the couple, only to find that they have already left. You thank the waiter, leave another tip, and head to the hotel to get some shut-eye.

The Journey, Day Four:

The next morning you wake up early and refreshed. You hop in the shower, brush your teeth, change your clothes, grab a bite to eat, and set out for the final phase of your journey. Around 11:00 p.m. that night, you finally arrive at your destination. You step out of your vehicle and take a long stretch. Before you can get your arms down, you are met with hugs and kisses from waiting family and friends. You take a moment to reflect on your journey and then quietly say to yourself, "I have arrived."

A simple analogy perhaps, but, in truth, events like these occur more than you realize. More importantly, however, the point here is that there was *someone, somewhere* who helped our traveler along the journey. The stranger, the automotive repair-shop manager, and the older couple were all very influential in assisting our traveler in reaching the destination.

Independent of the analogy, there was *someone, somewhere* who offered you an encouraging word as you were working hard to jump-start your career. Perhaps it was an associate or friend who witnessed your struggles and urged you to press forward and to not give up.

There was *someone, somewhere* who reached out to assist you when you were a student in college. Perhaps it was one of your professors or a fellow student who witnessed you experiencing difficulties in your calculus or statistics courses. These two subjects can be challenging for many students but can be overcome when students pull their mental resources together to achieve a common goal: completing the class with the best possible grade.

There was *someone, somewhere* who witnessed your desire and determination when you interviewed for your first management position. Perhaps the interviewers who stoically sat across the table from you after a long day of interviews saw just one leadership trait in you that made you stand out just slightly from the previous ten candidates who interviewed for the same position. Perhaps the interviewers had already made their final decision regarding who would be hired for the position; however, because you performed so well during the interview, they determined that you could be a better fit and decided to hire you for the position instead.

There was *someone, somewhere* who appreciated all of your hard work and effort on the job. Perhaps your boss came to you one day and said, "You have worked for me for many years and your performance has been consistently outstanding. I'd like to offer you a new position, and, by the way, it will be a promotion."

It is undeniable that there will always be *someone, somewhere*, standing in the gap to help you achieve your career goals and/or objectives. Good commonsense leaders understand that they do not operate in a vacuum. Our traveler, driving from Los Angeles to New York City, could have never finished the journey without the assistance and care of those who helped out.

Circling back to the introduction of this principle, many beginnings start from a humble position. It could be starting as a freshman in business school or as an hourly trainee to become the next frontline manager. The gleam in the eye tells a story of desire, strength, and determination to reach your career goals. You seek to gain knowledge from experienced and tenured leaders to help you on the path to achieve your career aspirations. Once you've reach your goal, you start to enjoy the fruits of your labor and never look back to those you helped you along the way. Your career has become your main focus, and you feel that you have "arrived," right?

Here's a thought: In truth, as long as you're in a leadership role and in command of human resources or human capital, be it personal or professional, *you will never* "arrive"! The absolute most noble thing an individual can do in life is to help others. As a leader, at home or at work, this will always be one of the most persistent issues in your entire life. Regardless of the endeavor, the human element will always pull at the very fiber of your emotional being (unless you're a robot).

The underlying message regarding this principle is this: to be an effective leader, **never forget your humble beginnings**. For many in leadership roles, this happens all too often; undoubtedly, it was good common sense that provided you the opportunity to achieve your aspirations and dreams in the first place. This dimension with regards to leadership teaching and training gets very little press and is rarely mentioned, but it is very important in shaping the comportments of future leaders.

The modern definition of *humbleness* involves weakness, but the truth is quite the contrary. From my experience, there are several characteristics I find more closely associated with humbleness than the modern definition:

- Humbleness is a sign of restraint, not passivity.
- Humbleness is a sign of strength, not weakness.
- Humbleness is a sign of intelligence, not incompetence.
- Humbleness is a sign of generosity, not narcissism.
- Humbleness is a sign of compassion, not intimidation.

Again, many leaders start from humble beginnings; however, it is increasingly important for good commonsense leaders to remain steadfast regarding this quality, particularly as you work to achieve your career goals and aspirations. This is a road that is truly less traveled but one that is more gratifying and fruitful in the sphere of human development.

I have met many individuals who I would consider great leaders throughout my life and career at various phases in their own personal journey. They all possessed a certain appeal—they were approachable and understanding, and they have a strong sense of valuing others.

Now perhaps many of these individuals may not consider themselves so great, but they gave me the impression that they have been in my shoes—a lasting impression that they had a fervent understanding of the many growing pains of becoming not only a great leader but also, and more importantly, a great person.

Whether you're a tenured or novice leader, it is important to understand that the skills and abilities you acquired to become an effective leader today will certainly help shape the future for the next generation of leaders. This is a truth that all leaders must be ever-cognizant of if we are to remain competitive and lead in the global arena.

Therefore, as leaders and as humans, it's important that we share good commonsense practices and principles because they are truly the foundation of a more structured and productive life.

XIII

The Noise-Pollution Principle

We live in a world where pollution can have a negative impact on the quality of life. There are several categories of pollutants: air, water, land, and noise. Each category, if not controlled or monitored, can produce harmful and adverse effects on human life.

Nations from around the globe have taken the effects of pollution very seriously. In the United States, the Environmental Protection Agency (EPA) was established to help protect human health and the environment from the effects that pollution can have on the quality of life.

From a principle perspective, noise pollution is undeniably the element most harmful to common sense. *Noise pollution, from a commonsense perspective, can run interference and distort the ability to pause and use sound judgment in most any situation.* Noise pollution has the ability to cloud the perpetual thought process essential to the natural commonsense conception; however, the fact of the matter is that it is somewhat difficult to avoid.

Our daily lives are bombarded with all kinds of noise from different media such as television, radio, work, play, and even at home. In addition, we can even place cellular phones in the category of noise producers.

The aforementioned mediums have the ability to influence the way we view life, our approach to problems or other situations, and the way we interact with others. Let's examine several cases in which noise producers interfered with the commonsense process, how common sense failed to prevail, and how it has impacted the lives of others.

Case One:
Where I live today, there have been four incidents this year of road rage that resulted in the death of innocent drivers. In one incident, the simple act of commuting took a deadly turn simply because one driver would not give way to the other who was attempting to get into the flow of traffic; a shouting match ensued because one driver accidentally bumped the other driver's vehicle. In these cases, not all of the perpetrators have been apprehended but those who have been are now facing years of incarceration.

Case Two:
We have witnessed several incidents in which protestors at a campaign rally were attacked and some injured simply because

they did not agree with the other person's political stance or belief. Many of the accused have been arrested and charged with battery.

Case Three:
In my hometown, at a major-league baseball game between crosstown rivals, two individuals got into an argument over the outcome of the game. The exchange got so heated that a fight ensued, and one person was severely injured. The individual accused of causing severe injuries to the other person was sentenced to jail because of his actions.

Case Four:
Research has already been done regarding this issue: Check with your local or state law enforcement agencies to determine the number of fatalities that occur each year that involve cellular phone usage while driving. Many states have outlawed the use of cell phones while driving motorized vehicles and have mandated that all cell-phone usage while driving be hands-free. In addition, many states have forbidden the use of cell phones when crossing intersections due to the number of fatalities and injuries that have occurred due to pedestrians using cell phones while crossing the street.

As you can see, in each of these cases, common sense was completely distorted and did not prevail, thus changing the lives of those left behind to deal with the outcome of those who failed to use good judgment.

In each case, many of the life-changing events were undoubtedly snap decisions that were made very quickly, which led to a less-than-desirable ending. The simple act of pausing and reflecting on the ramification of one's actions could have changed the results of each case. I can only surmise that the individuals who are now incarcerated wish that they had made a better choice.

As mentioned earlier, "Common sense is the basic ability to make decisions using sound judgment by way of an active, perpetual thought process that guides an individual through the decision-making process." There are many ways to exercise our common sense and help reduce the noise pollution that can hinder our ability to assess situations more clearly:

1. Try taking a leisurely walk in the park with a loved one, meditating on the good things about your life.
2. Spend time with family and friends and reflect on life's journey.
3. Turn off the television and partake of a good book with a positive message.
4. Connect with your spiritual side.
5. Start a workout routine. It doesn't have to be strenuous, just thirty minutes a day.

These and many other exercises can help you develop a more positive outlook on life and are very effective in feeding the natural senses. You may find other methods but the idea is to move your comportment beyond the narrative and the negative effects that noise pollution can have on your life.

You may never completely eliminate noise pollution as it relates to common sense—it is embedded in our everyday lives. However, you can reduce or influence the negative effects that it has on your life by constant practice and exercise of good commonsense principles. Take steps to shape the events in your life; don't let life events shape you.

XIV

A Closing Message

We have touched on several topics from a leadership and personal perspective regarding the dimensions and applications of the "Commonsense Approach." There are several themes that can be surmised from our discussion; however, there are two core purposes that I would like to identify as a quick reference to help move your internal compass in a more blissful direction:

- *The idea behind the commonsense approach is to be driven by an active thought process, not the moment.*
- *The purpose is designed to move the commonsense thought process past inertia into a realm that produces a more fruitful and rewarding life, regardless of the endeavor.*

As mentioned at the onset, common sense is an attribute that nearly all of us possess. It's a trait that is truly a part of our identity and can be impactful to the way we approach situations. It has the ability to affect our interactions with each other. Moreover, the use of good common sense has to be deliberate. It's a basic phenomenon of humans that has the ability to influence the success or failure of life's journey.

There will always be challenges in life that will transition us from one position to the next. For some, challenges have a way of bringing out the best in us and serving as a rudder to help steer us in the right direction. And for others, challenges can become daunting and at times overwhelming and have the ability to produce an inappropriate response of which the end result could prove detrimental to one's life or the lives of others. Both scenarios are at opposite ends of the spectrum, but in either case, common sense plays a key role to achieve a more positive and productive result.

As a leader, if you have found your rudder, continue on the northern trajectory. Deploying a commonsense strategy in all endeavors will prove critical, particularly as your reach higher to achieve your career or personal goals. Be mindful that challenges will accompany your dreams and aspirations, but that's okay; deploying good common sense in all aspects will always help you prevail.

If you have not found your rudder but are working assiduously to find it, I implore you to continue the search; by virtue, you will find it. Remember, challenges will come and go, but how you respond will ultimately make the difference in the quality of life shared by you and those who surround you as you continue the journey.

And finally, remember that your life can do a complete U-turn in a matter of seconds. You can be at the height of your career or position in life one moment and be faced with daunting challenges the next. Therefore, consume life and all the good and marvelous things it has to offer; don't let life consume you.

References

Gregoric, Pavel. *Aristotle on the Common Sense.* New York: Oxford University Press, 2007.

Lapowsky, Issie. "10 Things Employees Want Most." *Inc.*, August 27, 2010. http://www.inc.com/guides/2010/08/10-things-employees-want.html.

Moawad, Bob. *Whatever It Takes: A Journey into the Heart of Human Achievement.* Edmonds, WA: Compendium, 1998.

"The Pareto Principle, 80-20 Rule." Investopedia video, 2:23. April 30, 2015. http://www.investopedia.com/video/play/pareto-principle-8020-rule/#ixzz43TBuKaWk.

About the Author

Steven C. Duncan holds a BSM degree from National-Louis University in Lisle, Illinois. He has worked in management for twenty-eight years, holding positions in such organizations as FedEx, CRST International, and IDEXX Laboratories.

Duncan is a US Army veteran of six years and is currently pursuing an MBA from National-Louis University.

www.ingramcontent.com/pod-product-compliance
Lightning Source LLC
Chambersburg PA
CBHW070050210526
45170CB00012B/654